This Composition Book Belongs To:

____

ALL YOU NEED IS

LOVE

AND A

DOG

Made in United States
North Haven, CT
20 March 2022

17379803R00057